**Silly Signs and Offbeat Stuff
From America's Two-Lane Roads**

Remember traveling the historic Route 66? Did you ever make a cross-country old U.S. Route 40 -- the National Highway? Have you ever considered driving north to south along picturesque U.S. 41, from the Upper Peninsula of Michigan to the Atlantic Ocean at Miami Beach?

Loren Eyrich has made those trips, and many more. Fiddle-footed and free-spirited Loren devotes about six months a year to traveling and researching articles for his on-the-road newspaper, *Two-Lane Roads*.

In order to increase his own enjoyment of traveling, and also to discover fodder for his popular newspaper, Loren travels only the backroads, ignoring the tempting but boring stretches of high-speed interstate highway.

Along the way, he has photographed unusual, eyecatching -- and sometimes downright silly -- highway-oriented signs.

One such sign, warning people not to sleep on the pavement, became the title of this book.

Hundreds of other equally silly and nostalgic signs are offered here for your amusement.

Silly Signs and Offbeat Stuff
From America's Two-Lane Roads
BY LOREN EYRICH

Copyright © 1998 by Loren Eyrich

All rights reserved. No part of this book may be reproduced in any form without permission from the publisher, except in the case of quotations embodied in critical articles and reviews.

First printing 1998

Printed in the United States of America

No Sleeping On Pavement
Silly Signs and Offbeat Stuff
From America's Two-Lane Roads

ISBN # 0-937877-30-1

Cottage Publications, Inc.
420 S. Fourth Street
Elkhart, Indiana 46516-2748
(219) 293-7553

CONTENTS

		PAGE
About the Author		4
Chapter 1	Shunpiking	7
Chapter 2	Rural Mailboxes	12
Chapter 3	Juxtaposition	17
Chapter 4	Eat Here, Get Gas	23
Chapter 5	Miss Spelling's English Class Dropouts	30
Chapter 6	Smallest.....and Largest.....	37
Chapter 7	Ain't You Et Yet?	45
Chapter 8	Regional Food	51
Chapter 9	Outhouse Collections and Other Notable Attractions	57
Chapter 10	Roadside Nostalgia	73
Chapter 11	Just Plain Silly!	79
Chapter 12	Roadside Potpourri	107
Chapter 13	Road Ends	111

About the Author

Loren Eyrich spent 20 years in corporate America, as comptroller of Ed Morse Chevrolet in Fort Lauderdale, and also Lauderhill Leasing, Inc. Thanks mainly to a fleet of tens of thousands of cars sold and leased to companies like Alamo Rent-A-Car, Ed Morse was at that time the world's largest auto dealer.

In 1987, Loren walked away from a generous salary, the company car, paid health insurance, the walnut desk and a staff of 40 for a solitary life on the road in a weathered motorhome he calls the Condo-On-Wheels, or COW. The 1968 vintage camper body sits on a 1982 GMC cab & chassis, with 198,000 miles on the odometer. Loren lives in the camper about half of every year (six weeks on the road, six weeks at a home without wheels, four trips per year.)

Loren Eyrich at a campsite in South Carolina.

While the motorhome is old, it has modern conveniences such as generator, air conditioning, furnace, microwave, refrigerator, hot and cold water, plus the cameras and a Pentium computer needed to produce his on-the-road newspaper, *Two-Lane Roads* quarterly.

Loren eschews the interstates, driving almost exclusively on secondary highways. His six years of publishing have taken him to all states from Maine to Texas, and from Florida to Idaho. His only travel companion is a 17-year-old cat, Princess, who has adjusted quite well to traveling.

Condo-On-Wheels (COW) on the Old Lincoln Highway, Gap, Pennsylvania.

Princess, the cat who went to college.

For more information about *Two-Lane Roads* quarterly, subscription info, back issues available, plus information on the RV lifestyle, and ordering RV lifestyle books, please visit our website: http://www.two-lane.com

or write to:
**Two-Lane Roads
PO Box 23518
Fort Lauderdale, FL 33307-3518**

You may also contact Loren by phone, but remember that he's on the road half the year, so you may need to leave a message on his machine.
1-888-TWO-LANE

You can also meet Loren each year at major RV shows -- Florida RV Supershow, Tampa, January, and Pennsylvania RV and Camping Show, Harrisburg, September. Loren has also been an instructor at the Life On Wheels Conferences on RVing, held at the University of Idaho and extension courses nationwide.

To my dad

Dedicated to my dad, Ronald Eyrich (1909-1994.) For those Sunday afternoon drives in the country, for family vacations, for courage and patience while teaching me to drive; for your encouragement to explore America.

Chapter 1
Shunpiking

Shun-pike \n (1853):
A side road used to avoid the toll, speed, and traffic of a turnpike.
Shun-pik-ing:
Avoiding the superhighways, seeking out the scenic route instead.

At my booth at the Tampa RV show I was handing out sample issues of my newspaper, *Two-Lane Roads*. I handed one to a young woman, probably early 20s. Giving her my pitch, I said, "It's a quarterly publication. I stay off the interstates and visit the real America on two-lane roads."

US 30 snakes through the Allegheny Mountains, Pennsylvania.

She stared at the paper for a moment, then looked at me, and asked, "Why?"

"Well, because when you drive the interstate highways, all you see is the taillights of the big trucks as they go by. If you drive the two-lane roads, you might experience the real America," I replied.

Never any confusion on a two-lane road!

She stared at me for a moment, then looked at the paper for another moment, and looked back at me and asked, "So what is your point exactly?"

And I realized that girl and I were born in different generations. See, an entire generation of people has grown up on interstate highways, toll roads and freeways. Every time they get in the family car with Mom or Dad, the kids are taught that we are late, and we are in hurry. Mom heads for the freeway and curses when traffic refuses to move at the speed limit, or faster. Dad uses one finger to express displeasure at a driver who cuts in front of him. We need to get from Point A to Point B just as quickly as possible. That's our goal.

Things were different when I was a lad. Moms and dads would pile the kids in the car and go for a leisurely Sunday afternoon drive. There was no destination; the family would enjoy every mile of the outing. It was entertainment, and it was an education. Mom packed a picnic basket, and we'd find a roadside table and eat our lunch. We kids would play by the creek. We'd gather sticks and build a small fire in the grill and toast marshmallows. Back on the road, we'd enjoy the unique rural mailboxes. One farmer would set the post in an old milk bucket. The next might hang the mailbox by rope from the branch of a huge cottonwood tree. The dairy farmer painted his mailbox to resemble his Jersey cows. We kids would have a game to see who could spot the greatest number of out-of-state license plates.

Summer vacations found us exploring other regions of our country. We'd visit state parks, and we'd stop and read the historic markers placed along the roadway. We'd visit faraway places such as Washington D.C., where we watched Congress in action. We saw where the Pilgrims landed and where drunks slept in the streets of New York City. It wasn't Disney World; it was the Real World!

Al Hart keeps the Burma Shave legend alive with replica signs along US 30, Indiana.

Long before the concrete theme parks were built, there were Mom & Pop roadside attractions. A man spent his entire life collecting Indian arrowheads from his farm, and now he displayed them in his barn -- I mean museum -- for a fee. His wife weaved rugs and displayed them for sale by the highway.

Owners of roadside businesses dreamed up ways to attract Sunday drivers. Ice cream stores were shaped like a huge ice cream cone. Drive-in root beer stands offered service to our car. The waitress would appear on roller skates, hook the tray to our car window, and we'd enjoy a burger and root beer without ever leaving the comfort of Dad's Plymouth!

As we toured America, we'd find some ingenious advertising campaigns. In the Southeast, we'd watch for the red, black and white "See Rock City" barns. Or the thousands of billboards leading up to "South of the Border," Dillon, South Carolina. Nationwide, the Mail Pouch Tobacco barns. But the granddaddy of all roadside advertising had us kids watching the roadside for the next set of verses:

> "In school zones
> Take it slow,
> Let the little
> Shavers grow.
> Burma-Shave"

Today's interstate highways have been "cleansed" of all the color of the American people. Every mile, and every exit, looks the same. The late Charles Kuralt said it best: "Thanks to the interstate highway system, it is now possible to drive from coast to coast without seeing anything."

Now the good news. Most of the big trucks, and much of the heavy traffic, has been diverted to the interstate highways. And most of those two-lane roads we remember from the 1960s -- they still exist. Sometimes the old highway parallels the freeway, so we can tour the country on two-lane roads, yet as we approach a huge city, we might want to switch to the interstate just for a while.

So put your La-Z-Boy in overdrive, and join me as we tour backroads America. Let me warn you, parts of this book are pretty silly. If you were looking for some serious reading, you bought the wrong book! -L.E.

Chapter 2
Rural Mailboxes

You won't see a mailbox on America's interstate highways. Not one -- not ever! You need to drive the two-lane roads to see rural mailboxes. Many people show their artistic side as they personalize their mailboxes to identify their occupation, or their hobbies. Take a few minutes to enjoy our rural mailbox section. -L.E.

Right:
The owner makes a subtle statement about incoming mail.
U.S. 1, Maine

Above: I love mailboxes which seem to defy the laws of gravity, "hanging" from a chain!

Left: This is NOT Tunnel Mountain Road, and I'm tired of getting his bills!
Silva, North Carolina

Above: Even an automobile crankshaft is recycled.

Right: Mom's old wringer washing machine finds new life.

Right: "Uncle Sam wants YOUR letters!"

Below: A fisherman's mailbox

Right: A mailbox can tell people about your favorite pastime.
Florida

HOTMAIL!

Above: And the old plow.

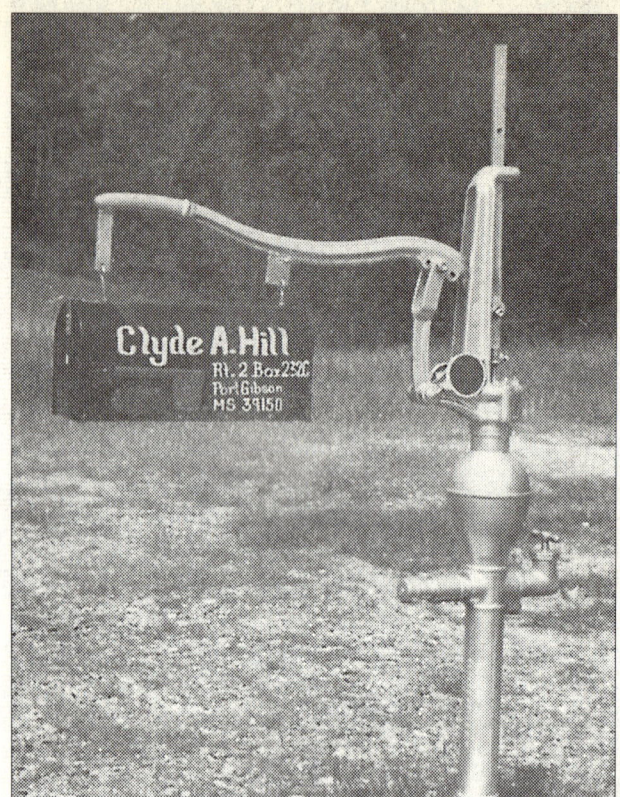

Make use of that old water pump.

Port Gibson, Mississippi

Cow mailboxes are very popular (and cute.)

Chapter 3
Juxtaposition

Juxtaposition \n (1665):
　The act or an instance of placing two or more things side by side.

Juxtapose \vt (1851):
　To place side by side unexpected combination of colors, shapes, and ideas.

Imagine, two towns in South Carolina: Clinton, South Carolina. Prosperity, South Carolina. Not particularly funny, is it?

Now, imagine Clinton and Prosperity on one sign, with arrows pointing in opposite directions. Either sign by itself, benign. Juxtapose the two, and suddenly, it becomes hilarious! And with that in mind, I present the next group of signs, Juxtaposition. -L.E.

Two towns in Sourth Carolina.

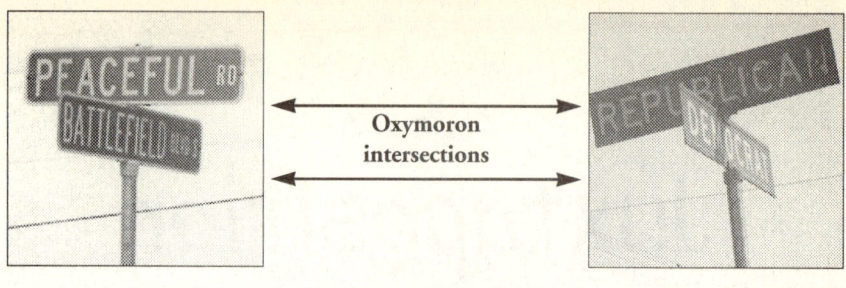

Oxymoron intersections

Left: There is one primary place in North America where crocodiles are found in the wild -- the coastal waters of southeast Florida. The lake was named not by someone surprised by a crocodile, but by builders of the Florida East Coast Railway, when they found a lake in their path, not charted by the surveyors.

U.S. 1, Key Largo, Florida

Eat healthy -- or not. Either way, the Wagner family is here to help. Wagner's Health Foods, Wagner Funeral Home.

U.S. 169, south of Minneapolis

Above: Fishing Bridge was named in 1914 for the excellent fishing here. Trouble is, fishing in this cutthroat trout spawning ground was just too easy, and threatening the species. Since 1973, there is "no fishing" on fishing bridge!
Yellowstone National Park, Wyoming

Below: Two towns in Idaho (neither has a University).

Above: I didn't even know he was sick!
Memphis, Tennessee

Right: Harry Houdini grew up in Appleton, Wisconsin, which named a street in his honor. But don't you think Houdini would have found a challenge in the "No Outlet" status of his street?
Downtown Appleton, Wisconsin

Above: And what lady doesn't love a peanut boil?
U.S. 90, Northern Florida

Right: Outlet only. No, maybe it's the entrance to the outlet.
Maine

They're open. Nope, they're closed!

One-stop shopping. Rent a video, go hunting.
U.S. 441, Clayton, Georgia

One-stop shopping. Rent a video, and go fishing.
Georgia

Chapter 4
Eat Here, Get Gas

In this chapter, we examine signs which have a double meaning. Some years back, the owner of a truck stop wanted to increase his business. Drivers would surely enjoy the convenience of his one-stop truck stop, if only they knew about it in advance. Folks whizzing by at 70 mph didn't have time to read, "We have one-stop convenience, a restaurant and a gas station." So the truck stop owner erected this sign:

EAT HERE
GET GAS

And people stopped. They did enjoy the one-stop convenience. Other truck stops followed suit, hoping to attract more business. All was fine until a tourist with a camera snapped the photo and sent it to a newspaper or magazine. The editor saw the double meaning and decided to publish the photo. People photographed other examples of the same sign, and it would be published in additional periodicals.

And so "Eat Here, Get Gas" has became an American standard, a classic example of a sign with multiple interpretations.

I must admit that in six years of scouring America's two-lane roads for news stories, I have yet to find an example of an "Eat Here, Get Gas" sign. The closest I've come was a billboard for a truck stop in Alabama which advertised, "Free meal with 100 gallons of gas." How I was wishing they would shorten it to, "Free food with gas." That would have been a photo opportunity!

Here's another I spotted in North Carolina:

JODY'S
USED TIRES
6.00 AND UP
GUARANTEED
1 MILE

Now, I am inclined to think that 50% of drivers who see this sign don't even give it a second glance. Their brain processes it and comes back, "Well, the sign tells us Jody sells used tires, and they are guaranteed, and he is located 1 mile ahead. Why is that funny?"

The other 50% of us say, "That's hilarious! He intended to tell us he is located one mile ahead, but the sign could be interpreted as the tires are guaranteed for one mile. Now that's funny!"

Strongest guarantee in the tire business!
U.S. 301, North Carolina

My question is, was Jody as naive as we imagine? Or is he an advertising genius? Perhaps -- just perhaps -- he planned this sign fully aware that its double meaning would attract attention. Is he oblivious to the humor, or is he laughing all the way to the bank?

With that in mind, this chapter is titled, "Eat Here, Get Gas." -L.E.

Who would buy a tire knowing it May Pop?
Mississippi

And yes, I have eaten at D&H Barbecue, and I highly recommend it. Only very rarely do patrons require a trip to the hospital next door!

Manning, South Carolina

And residents -- they are encouraged to dump their garbage?

Old Town, Florida

Sometimes it may be better not to follow instructions literally.

Left: Drive through the flowers?
Below: Drive through the window?

Hurry, last chance to get drunk before the turnpike!
Pennsylvania Turnpike entrance

Sorry Clarabell, you'll have to go.
A campground in Saco, Maine, which doesn't allow pets, except for the owner's pet burro.

But officer, the pavement is too smooth!
Minnesota

Toys??

Right: Younger folks may park right out front.
Dixie Highway, Oakland Park, Florida

Left: From the, "Do we really need to tell people this?" department.
Florida

Have you noticed Carl's wife seems to be a lot happier lately?
North Florida

All bears must register!
Florida

And then...?
Lincoln Highway, U.S. 30, Pennsylvania

Chapter 5

Miss Spelling's English Class Dropouts

O r, "You say potato, I say potatoe." The Dan Quayle chapter. I empathize with these people. Were it were not for my computer's spell checker, I would be worse than any of these! -L.E.

Left: "Miss Spelling's English class."

Right: Granny wasn't sure, so she spelled "burgers" two different ways, figuring she had a 100% chance of being correct 50% of the time.
Maggie Valley, North Carolina

Above: Why can't our kids spell? Could it be because the high school administrators can't spell either?

Gilbert, South Carolina

And don't "ote" for the same "urkeys" you elected last time!

Williston, Florida

Left: Prime waterfront lots on a "canel."

Florida Keys

Above: More prime waterfront property, with "akcess" to the Gulf!

Tarpon Springs, Florida

Right: Sign with dyslexia.

Myrtle Beach, South Carolina

I guess the property is near the railroad tracks?

Somewhere in Florida

Right: Love that "sweaty" barbecue!

Left: Sometime in the "passed," you "past us!"

I'll bet it's pretty good for carving, too.
Santa Rosa, Florida

It's so "cheep" it's birdseed!

Left and below: I can never remember how to spell business, either.

Chapter 6
Smallest... and Largest...

Nearly every little town in America has some claim to fame, usually posted near the town limits:

"Frog capitol of the world" -Rayne, Louisiana
"America's sweetest town" -Clewiston, Florida
"Peach capital of the world" -Johnson, South Carolina
"Sweet onion city" -Vidalia, Georgia
"Easternmost point in the USA" -Lubec, Maine
"The center of the universe" -Ashland, Virginia
"Sweet corn capital of the world" -Hoopeston, Illinois
"Cleanest city in Texas" -Shiner, Texas
"Too beautiful to burn." (quote by Gen. U.S. Grant) -Port Gibson, Mississippi
"Birthplace of Elvis Presley" -Tupelo, Mississippi
"Birthplace of Paul Bunyan" -Bemidji, Minnesota
"World's largest ball of twine" (rolled by one man) -Darwin, Minnesota
"Sam Walton's first store" -Bentonville, Arkansas

OK, now before you write letters, I know there are probably at least a dozen towns that claim to be the peach capital of the world. I am reporting only what I see; the claim made by each of these towns. As far as I know, there is no certification process required for the towns to post these claims. I have not measured every church in the world; yet I have no reason to believe the one in Bayou Goula, Louisiana, is not the world's smallest, as claimed. If you suspect that there is a town that should have the title of "Catfish Capital" or "smallest city hall" or you don't believe Bill Clinton was really born in Hope, Arkansas, then I suggest you write to the chambers of commerce. You can write me if you want, but it won't do you any good. -L.E.

America's Smallest Post Office: Ochopee, Florida

Yes, this is official, and documented by the US Postal Service. The steel building, a former irrigation pump shed, approximately 7 x 8 feet, was pressed into service in 1953, when the post office and general store burned down and has been in service ever since.

Back in the 1930s, Ochopee was a booming town, surrounded by cypress logging camps, 8 sawmills, and tomato farming and packing industry. Rail lines criss-crossed the region, and steam locomotives hauled out the lumber, which was used worldwide for ship building. Lumbering continued through the 1950s, until the cypress forest was nearly stripped bare.

America's smallest post office.
Ochopee, Florida

Today, the region is protected as part of Big Cypress National Preserve. The tiny post office serves about 400 local patrons, most of them Seminole and Miccosukee Indians and employees of the Big Cypress Preserve. The working post office is open weekdays; Postmaster Naomi Lewis is kept really busy when tour buses stop, and dozens of European visitors wait in line to buy a postcard of America's smallest post office and to have it postmarked Ochopee, Florida USA.

In 1995 Collier County designated Ochopee's post office a Historic Site.

US 41, Tamiami Trail, east of State Road 29, Ochopee, Florida

World's Smallest Church -- Madonna Chapel
Bayou Goula, Louisiana

I've seen other churches which claim to be "smallest church in the USA," "smallest church in 48 states," "smallest cathedral," but so far, this appears to be the winner. For the record, it's about 8 x 12 feet, with seating for 6. At least one mass is celebrated annually, making it a real church. Chapel of the Madonna was built in 1903 by an Italian immigrant sugar farmer named Anthony Gullo. His son became deathly ill, and Gullo prayed to the Virgin Mary, promising to build a church if the child survived. He did, and so Gullo built the chapel as he vowed.

The church is locked, but you'll find the key in the mailbox. Please lock the door when you leave, and place the key in the mailbox so that others may enjoy it.

State Road 405 just north of Bayou Goula, Louisiana

World's smallest church -- Madonna Chapel
Bayou Goula, Louisiana

World's smallest police station

This little town has just two police cars, and when they're not on patrol, you'll generally find one of them parked beside this police station. Inside is the official police phone -- a direct line to the police dispatcher. A few years back the town had an incident involving two suspects. One of the police officers apprehended one suspect and handcuffed him to the police station, then continued on to round up the other suspect. He then returned and transported both suspects to the county jail.

U.S. 98, town center
Carrabelle, Florida

World's largest catsup bottle.

When the Brooks catsup company talked of scrapping its old water tower, the townspeople wouldn't hear of it. A restoration committee was formed and donations poured in, saving the town landmark.

Collinsville, Illinois.
S.R. 159 south of town.

World's largest Mr. Peanut statue.
Planter's Peanut plant, U.S. 71, south of Fort Smith, Arkansas.

World's largest turkey.
Frazee, Minnesota, in town park.

World's largest loon (Minnesota's state bird)

*Loon Lake,
near Vergas, Minnesota.*

Above: World's largest 6-pack.
Storage for 22,000 barrels of beer, or 7,340,796 cans. That would provide one person a six-pack a day for 3,351 years!

Heilman's Old Style Brewery, U.S. 61, Great River Road, LaCrosse, Wisconsin.

World's largest prairie chicken.
C.R. 52 and visible from I-94, Rothsay, Minnesota.

Chapter 7
Ain't You Et Yet?

Folks driving the interstate highways see the same food at every exit. It's as if someone came down the highway with a big rubber stamp. "McDonalds," "Subway," "Red Lobster," "Taco Bell," "Olive Garden," "Wendy's." Folks feel comfortable eating at these establishments because the menu is exactly the same at every one, worldwide. Mind you, it's good food; my argument is if you are going to eat at the same restaurant every night, you may as well stay home!

Ain't You Et Yet Cafe -- Excellent pinto beans and cornbread

U.S. 60, between Charleston and Fayetteville, West Virginia

Folks driving from Point A to Point B on the interstate will never have the pleasure of sampling regional foods, like: Cajun food at Sweet P's, Rayne, Louisiana; McCabe's family barbecue, Manning, South Carolina; soul food at J.B.'s Place, Port Gibson, Mississippi; Maine lobster at Seawall Restaurant, Bar Harbor, Maine; Tex-Mex food at Chentes Restaurant, Alice, Texas; Caputo's Pizza, Dry Tavern, Pennsylvania; catfish at Homecoming Restaurant, Thomasville, Georgia; Breitbach's tavern (Iowa's oldest), Balltown, Iowa; buffet at Five Forks Inn, Tionesta, Pennsylvania; Amish home cooking, Boyd & Wurthmann Restaurant, Berlin, Ohio.

I highly recommend the above restaurants. The signs appearing on the following pages are not necessarily an endorsement. If they serve good food, I'll tell you. If they don't, or if I didn't try the food, I will print nothing. -L.E.

**Custer's Last Root Beer Stand --
Smooth, creamy root beer in
frosted mugs.**

*U.S. 287,
Three Forks, Montana*

**I Ain't Here Saloon -- (Has since been
renamed Marie's Nut House)**

*U.S. 19/27/98
Old Town, Florida*

**Interior walls in No Name Pub are covered in dollar bills. Autograph the bill,
stick it on the wall.**

On No Name Road, No Name Key, Florida Keys.

Above: Clever play on words in this mining region.

U.S. 287 near Jeffrey City, Wyoming

The "Original" Hard Rock Cafe, Empire, Colorado

Named long before hard rock music, even long before rock & roll, this Hard Rock Cafe was named in 1934 for the hard rock mining common in this region of Colorado.

The more well-known Hard Rock Cafes began much later; the first in London in 1971. And yes, the larger company has tried at least once to sue the little cafe to stop using the name. A former owner of the cafe, realizing he wouldn't have the resources needed to fight that lawsuit, assigned the name to the City of Empire, Colorado, and the "big boys" from London dropped the suit, fearing they could never win against an entire city. They probably never bothered to check, but the entire city of Empire, Colorado is only 432 residents.

Good sandwiches.

US 40, Empire, Colorado

Left: Wonder if Wimpy can order a hamburger today and pay for it tomorrow?

Above: Hey, I resemble that name!

Left: No doubt those heavy pedestrians just came from the Big Belly Deli.

Right: Dirty Shame Saloon, Yaak, Montana

Good sandwiches.

*Yaak River Rd. (C.R. 508)
Yaak, Montana*

Desert Inn --
Yeehaw Junction, Florida

Built around 1889, on the National Register of Historic Places. Late in the last century, cowboys rode the flat terrain of Florida, rounding up scrub cattle -- offspring of cattle abandoned here by the Spanish explorers. To get the attention of a wayward cow, the Florida cowboys would "crack" their leather whips, hence the name, "Florida Cracker."

They'd drive the cattle to ports near Fort Myers, where the cattle would be shipped off to Cuba. Paid in gold, the cowboys had currency far more valuable than the government money in post-Civil War Florida.

At the end of a spur on the Florida East Coast Railway, a station was built. Cowboys would sell cattle and buy supplies, including jackasses for various ranch duties. The town became called Jackass Crossing, and the Desert Inn was a saloon and gambling hall for the cowboys. It was as tough a crowd as any town in America's wild West.

Legend says that when the first highway was built through Jackass Crossing, Standard Oil wanted to place a service station in the town, but the oil company objected to the town name. And so, the town was renamed to the sound a jackass makes, Yeehaw.

Good cheeseburgers, history, and fun. If there are ladies in your party, make certain they visit the ladies' room!

Junction US 441 & State Road 60 & Florida's Turnpike,
Yeehaw Junction, Florida

In a region dominated by fish restaurants, T-bones advertises "Catch of the day, cow."

U.S. 17 Murrells Inlet, South Carolina

He: "You want to meet somewhere for lunch?"

She: "I'd like that. Where should we meet?"

He: "A place to eat would be nice."

She: " Yes, smart guy, that would be nice. But what restaurant?"

He: "A place to eat."

She: "Never mind, smart ass, I'll eat by myself."

Downtown Conway, Arkansas

Chapter 8
Regional Food

This is road food, but found only in specific regions of America. -L.E.

Below: Wow, watch orange juice being squeezed right before your eye! And who says there are no free attractions anymore?

U.S. 301, north Florida

Only in Maine.

Only in Massachusetts.

Pony "Espresso" Station
U.S. 287, Dubois, Wyoming

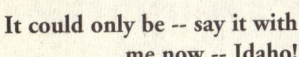

It could only be -- say it with me now -- Idaho!

Along every highway...
Boiled peanuts are a favorite snack in the Southeast. Boiled in salt water, they become soft, like salty cooked beans.

U.S. 27, Lake Hamilton, Florida

In Dan's hometown, Huntington, Indiana.

It's not pronounced "PAY-stees" but "PAST-ees" and they are similar to meat pies. Irish immigrants who worked the copper mines in upper Michigan found that their lunches would become damp and cold by lunch time. Their wives sewed special pockets inside the men's pants; then baked the meat and potatoes pies, and placed them in the men's pants. At lunch time, the pasties were a warm treat!

U.S. 41, Michigan's Upper Peninsula

Holy Cow Ice Cream
U.S. 9 West, New York State

Everyone knows what they eat in Wisconsin.

Butt meat, liver puddin', and hog head cheese. Yummm. Bake them into pasties, and stuff them in your pants!

South Carolina

Chapter 9

Outhouse Collections and Other Notable Attractions

You all know about America's huge theme parks. You can visit them on the interstates. But if you would like to see the REAL America, visit the little-known museums, where Mom and Pop are the curators. Many of these people have spent their entire adult lives collecting the artifacts for your perusal. Overlook them, and you will miss an opportunity to meet some of the most colorful people our nation has. -L.E.

Why travel to New York City and Philadelphia when you can see BOTH the Statue of Liberty AND the Liberty Bell in one place!

Town center, McRae, Georgia

All: Frog capital of the world, and Louisiana's city of murals. Dozens of frog murals are seen around town. Even the fire hydrants are frogs.

U.S. 90, Rayne, Louisiana

Solomon's Castle -- Howard Solomon is the self-proclaimed "Rembrandt of Reclamation" and the "DaVinci of Debris." Solomon claims he was sold the 55-acre tract in the winter dry season, unaware that it was in the flood plain of Horse Creek and would flood every summer! Undaunted, he built a levee and installed pumps. Then the self-taught carpenter, plumber and electrician designed and built a magnificent castle. He never drew any plans on paper! Nearly the entire castle is made from discarded materials. The exterior is sheathed in used metal printing plates. As the clouds pass overhead, the silver castle changes colors, like a hologram. There are 80 stained-glass windows, each telling a story; either a fairy tale, or Bible story.

During a $5 tour, Howard shows guests the thousands of art objects he's made entirely from discarded materials. He holds up a short piece of 2x4 lumber. "I invented the pet block," Howard begins. "Amazingly, it is cut from a single piece of wood!" Howard doesn't crack a smile, but waits patiently for the crowd to catch up with his quick wit. "Everything here is recycled; this was once a tree!"

From Zolfo Springs, State Road 64 west to Ona, Florida, south on CR 663.

Hy Goldenberg and his outhouse collection--
Years ago, Hy and Lorry Goldenberg were building a new home on the Wabash River, outside Huntington, Indiana (hometown of Dan Quayle.)

"I realized the workers would need a place to go before they could install the plumbing," Hy explains. "So I went down to Monument City, a town which had been condemned, as a dam was being built and the town would be flooded. I picked out what I thought was a colorful outhouse, like something from a Li'l Abner cartoon. I paid $2 for the outhouse, plus another $2 to have it delivered. When the truck pulled up at our place, I noticed there were two outhouses on it. The driver explained that I had picked out the worst outhouse in town, so he thought he better bring a better one. I explained that I purposely selected the worst outhouse. Anyway, I now had the start of a collection. Two of anything is a collection."

But Hy Goldenberg didn't stop at two. He traveled to auctions, and bid on additional outhouses. A round outhouse painted in barn red. A concrete outhouse, used by the railroads. A three-holer family outhouse. When I visited Hy, he had 14 outhouses, painted a variety of colors!

(Hy and Lorry have moved to a smaller home in town, and the outhouse collection is now under the care of their children and not open to the public.)

Petrified Wood Service Station--

A lumber dealer named W. G. Brown watched the steady stream of motorists heading west on US 50, Lamar, Colorado. Tourists rushed through town, eager to arrive at the well-publicized mountain regions to the west. For years Brown dreamed of creating a local tourist attraction to get them to stop. At last, the answer came to him.

And so he built a fireproof gas station, made entirely of wood. Flame resistant, 175,000,000 year-old petrified wood! Doors and windows are flanked by giant tree trunks, nearly 4 feet in diameter. The largest piece weighs 3,200 pounds. Even the doors are made of petrified wood.

His gas station was completed in 1932. And yes, motorists stopped for gas, and a picture for their scrapbook.

The old gas station is no longer in use, but it still stands in the original spot, today part of Stagner Tire.

Oh, the wood is termite-proof and won't need painting for 175,000,000 years.

US 50 and US 287, Lamar, Colorado

Above:
Town Square, Mars, Pennsylvania

Cadillac Ranch--

Stanley Marsh III collected 10 Cadillac automobiles, vintage early 1950's, and buried them nose-down, tailfins up, in a field along US Route 66 west of Amarillo, Texas. Decades of visitors have stripped the cars of everything but the body shells and painted them with graffiti.

Route 66 has been buried beneath I-40. Still, the tourists come to Cadillac Ranch.

I-40 west of Amarillo, Hope Road exit, then east on frontage road.

Carhenge--

No one knows the origin of Carhenge. Some say ancient man created it as some astronomical timepiece. Just how were they able to move those huge boulders.... Wait a minute. Perhaps I am confusing this with Stonehenge. The "stones" which make up Carhenge are 1950-vintage Studebakers, Cadillacs, and Plymouths. Conceived by Jim Reinders, Carhenge was built in 1987 during a family reunion on a farm where Reinders once lived. Dozens of junk cars were buried, nose down, then others placed on top, carefully replicating the placement of stones at Stonehenge.

US 385, north of Alliance, Nebraska.

Kliment Studebaker Dealership--

The last Studebaker rolled off the assembly line in 1966, but don't tell Pete Kliment. His father opened the red brick garage in 1902, selling Chandler, Cleveland, and Hupmobile automobiles, before becoming a Studebaker dealer in 1935. When Studebaker quit building cars, most Studebaker dealers either retired, or found other brands of cars to sell. Pete stayed in business. He still has brand-new Studebaker replacement parts which he ships worldwide, and he restores Studebaker automobiles for collectors. In the showroom is a "new" 1950 Studebaker.

US 30, Greensburg, Pennsylvania

"Five Dollar" Frank Thomas--

For the small sum of money suggested by his nickname, "Five Dollar" Frank Thomas takes visitors for an airplane ride over the scenic New River Gorge. Frank doesn't need to wait for an air traffic controller to tell him when to take off and land. His airport has no air traffic controller. Frank Thomas owns the Fayette Airport.

Once airborne, Frank will recite original poetry, and tell you what is wrong with the government of West Virginia. He's an outspoken but loveable character who has taught over 1,000 pilots to fly. "Five of them flew in one squadron in Desert Shield." Frank says proudly.

Fayette Airport is south of the US 19 Bridge over the New River Gorge.
Fayetteville, West Virginia

Booger Hollow, Arkansas--

It's a great tourist trap, featuring Hillbilly souvenirs (examples: a "Hillbilly flashlight" is a match; a "Hillbilly washer and dryer" is a steel hardware washer glued to a clothespin); a snack bar, and Booger Hollow's famous two-story outhouse. "Top floor closed, until we figure out the plumbing." Booger Hollow is a politically INcorrect throwback to the tourist attractions of yesterday, and I love everything about it!

State Road 7 north of Russellville, Arkansas.

Haines Shoe House--

"Colonel" Mahlon N. Haines "made his fortune selling shoes. He was known as the Shoe Wizard," explains Mrs. Ruth R. Miller, current owner of Haines Shoe House. "He didn't build the house for himself; he would loan it out, free of charge, for special occasions, like birthdays, wedding anniversaries, and honeymoons. And he would include a maid, a car and even a chauffeur, all free!"

The people fortunate enough to stay at the shoe house were usually employees of the 40-some retail shoe stores in Haines' shoe empire. Haines had the house built in 1948. The shoe is 48 feet long, 17 feet wide, and 25 feet tall. Inside are three bedrooms, two baths, a kitchen and living room, on 5 levels. Every window in the shoe is stained glass, including one bearing Haines' likeness.

Haines Shoe House is visible from US 30, east of York, Pennsylvania. It's open for tours. Take the Hallam exit off Route 30, south to State Road 462 (Old Lincoln Highway) west on 462 and then north on Shoe House Road.

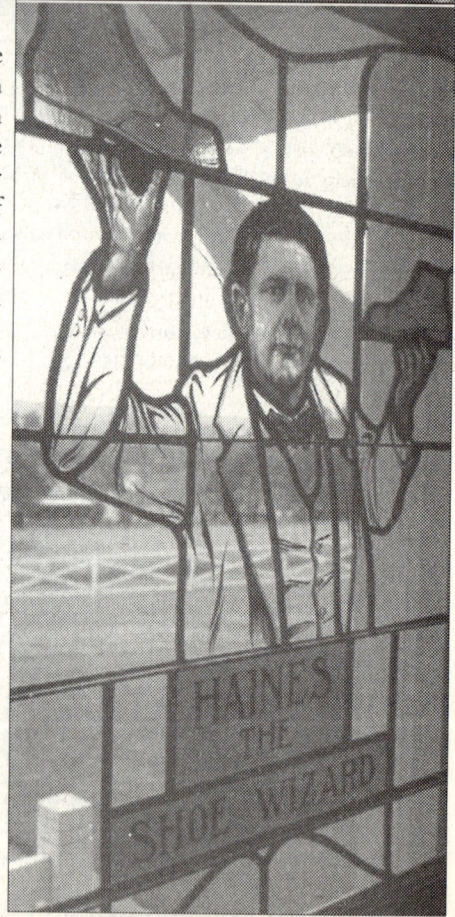

World's only Coon Dog Memorial Park--

Key Underwood established the cemetery back in 1937, when his coon hunting dog "Troop" passed away. Hundreds of dogs rest here, some of them in graves marked by marble stones. It's a lovely setting, on the crest of a hill, overlooking pine forests. But no ordinary dogs can be buried here. To qualify, they must be coon dogs, and they must have treed the minimum number of raccoons in their lifetimes.

Near Florence, Alabama

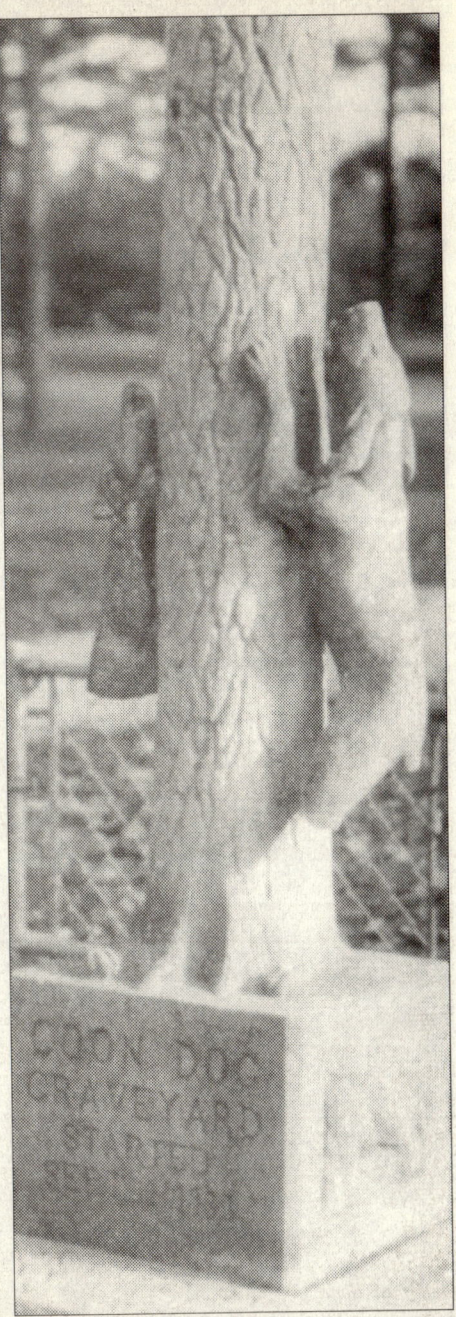

George Preston's Gas Station--

George Preston and his wife Blanche ran this gas station at this location on the Lincoln Highway since 1923. The collector of automobile memorabilia was probably the world's foremost authority on the historic Lincoln Highway (America's first trans-continental highway.) A great story teller, Preston was a frequent guest on the Tonight Show with Johnny Carson, entertaining the audience with his memories of the old days of the automobile. (George Preston died in 1993 at the age of 83; his gas station is closed.)

County Road E66 (Old Lincoln Highway) Belle Plaine, Iowa

**John Dolan,
Porcupine's Delight--**

John Dolan builds things from wood. His specialty, bat houses. "The bat is a misunderstood mammal," says Dolan, who encourages people to own a bat house to attract bats, which will rid your yard of mosquitoes.

*State Road 189 near US 1,
Whiting, Maine*

Henry's Museum of Horns, "The Horniest Place in Texas."

Over 5,000 deer antlers hang from the ceiling in this tavern.

Plantersville, Texas

Joe Bryant and the National Stove Museum--

Joe and Bea Bryant own an antique stove reconditioning facility and a stove museum. Joe is in charge of the repair shop, but when a tourist shows up, he just may take the remainder of the day off, choosing instead to show off his collection of antique player pianos, paper roll organs, and his Model-T Ford.

Thorndike, Maine

Miracle of America Museum, "The Smithsonian of the West."
One man's lifetime collection of Americana.

US 93 south of Polson, Montana.

World's only Boll Weevil Monument--

The insect killed the cotton industry, but not the spirit of the people of Enterprise, Alabama. Where they formerly depended on just one commodity, they now diversified; planting peanuts, and building a manufacturing industry to replace jobs lost in cotton fields. "In profound appreciation" the town erected a monument to the Boll Weevil!

Town Square, Enterprise, Alabama

Max Nordeen's Wheels Museum--

Max Nordeen has collected memorabilia from World's Fairs. From the 1876 Philadelphia World's Fair. And many others. He's got a stereo optical viewer with a picture of the largest Ferris Wheel ever built, for the Chicago World's Fair. It held 36 coaches, each holding 60 passengers! Plus he has 26 motor vehicles and 65 kid's pedal cars. And thousands of other items. For a tiny admission charge, he'll tell you the history of each and every object in the museum.

North of Woodhull, Illinois

Museum of Questionable Medical Devices

Founder and curator Bob McCoy has collected hundreds of devices which were at one time thought to be medical cures. Many have been seized by the FDA because they either do not provide the medical benefit claimed or in some cases they are downright dangerous. The Phrenology Machine is the bowl-shaped device which I'm wearing on my head. The inventor claimed that by measuring the shape of one's head, you could determine his personality traits. Sold as recently as 1935, the machine could generate a comfortable sum of money in department stores, theater lobbies, and county fairs.

They didn't work as promised, but at least they never killed anyone. Not so with some of the items in this "Museum of Quackery." Like foot X-ray machines, commonly used in shoe stores until banned in 1970. Or a radioactive tonic called Radithor. People bought it, and for a while, they did fine. One customer drank 3 bottles a day until he died of radium poisoning at 51. The promoter wasn't just a salesman, he was a client! He used the product himself until his death in 1949 of bladder cancer. When his body was exhumed 20 years later, his remains still set off a Geiger counter.

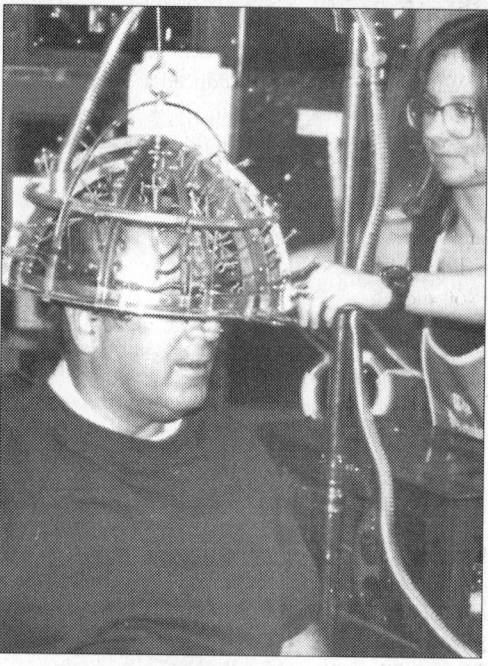

Loren gets his head examined by Christa M. Patterson at the Museum of Questionable Medical Devices.

Located at:
St. Anthony Main,
219 Main St. SE,
Minneapolis, Minnesota

World's largest Edsel collection--

When the Edsel was introduced as a 1958 model, the radical styling of the new car split Americans right down the middle. You either loved it, or you hated it! Pennsylvania farmer Hugh Lesley instantly fell in love with the Edsel, but knew he couldn't afford one.

History would show that Ford's timing in introducing the Edsel was a couple years late. America was in an automobile recession in 1958. Then for 1959 Ford softened the styling of the Edsel, and sales plummeted. Production ceased after just 3 months of the 1960 model.

Values of used Edsels dropped, and Hugh Leslie found he could finally afford one. And another one. And he's never stopped buying. At last count, he had 170 Edsels on his farm, most in pretty rough shape, but a few are gems!

Oxford, Pennsylvania (not open to the public)

Captain Tom O'Lenick--

Captain Tom runs a charter fishing boat on the Silver and Ocklawaha Rivers. The Silver flows from the famous Silver Springs area, joining the Ocklawaha, which flows to the St. Johns River. The river meanders through cypress forests. Tom sings to the fish, and entertains visitors with his tall fish stories.

State Road 40,
Silver Springs, Florida

"Preacher" and Margaret Dennis, Margaret's Grocery & Bible Class--
Margaret and her late husband opened the grocery store in 1952. Her husband died in the store; shot during a robbery. Years later, her children introduced her to Rev. H.D. "Preacher" Dennis. Margaret still operates the small grocery store, but Preacher has transformed the appearance. He's added bright red and white signs quoting Bible verses. He's brought in a vintage school bus, where 20 to 30 parishioners gather every Sunday to hear the preacher's sermon.

US 61 north of Vicksburg, Mississippi

Harvest Village--
Replica of an old gas station, plus a historic railroad station.
US 441, McIntosh, Florida

Chapter 10
Roadside Nostalgia

I hope as you look through these pictures, you will remember some road-trip of long ago. -L.E.

Mammy's Cupboard--
   Henry Gaude built this eye-catcher around 1940. It's been a beer joint, gas station, and restaurant. Nearly destroyed a few years back when the highway was widened, a few people lobbied to save the cute little building. The highway was diverted in order to save it from the bulldozers.
   Today it's owned by Doris Kemp, who operates Mammy's Cupboard, selling home-made food and crafts. -- *US 61 south of Natchez, Mississippi*

Twistee Treat Ice Cream--

U.S. 441, Okeechobee, Florida

Virlillia Store - since 1840s

If it has ever been painted, there surely isn't any evidence of paint on the boards now! It originally served the Cameron Plantation, just up the road. Ledgers in the store trace entries back to at least 1869. As recently as the 1950's, Virlillia was a busy town, with cotton gin and a movie theater. Today, the general store is all that is left of the town.

West of Canton, Mississippi on S.R. 22, bear to the right on Virlillia Road.

Evinston, Florida, Post Office, 1884--

Evinston was part of a Spanish land grant in 1817. Captain W.D. Evins had large land holdings here on the west shore of Orange Lake. A railroad station and this general store were built in 1884. At one time the town boasted two other stores, a school, three churches, a blacksmith shop, two produce packing houses, and a grist mill.

The store was built of heart pine, by W.P. Shettleworth. In 1909, the store was sold to H.D. Wood and Robert Evins. Then in 1934, to a partnership of Wood and Swink.

Fred Wood was postmaster, beginning in 1934 and continuing for the next 44 years. His daughter-in-law, Sue Wood, has been postmaster for all the years since. This post office has no delivery routes; each of the 83 boxholders comes to the post office to pick up mail. Most sit and talk for awhile. In the winter, they gather around the wood stove. Store ledgers go back to the first year of business.

The Evinston US Post Office is inside the Wood & Swink Store. To find the store, drive US 441 between McIntosh and Micanopi; follow the signs to Evinston.

See Rock City Barns--

Remember the "See Rock City" barns? If you traveled anywhere in the southeastern United States in the 1950s or 1960s, chances are you've seen hundreds of the barns, each with the roof or sides pained with white letters on black background, "See Rock City. See 7 states."

It all began in the 1920s, when Garnet and Frieda Carter developed a garden walkway on their estate atop Lookout Mountain, in northern Georgia, overlooking Chattanooga, Tennessee. America was in the Great Depression when the Carters opened their gardens to the public in 1932. In what would become one of the most creative and successful advertising gimmicks ever, Carter painted "See Rock City" on hundreds of barns located along highways leading to Chattanooga.

The barns are so cherished by America's baby boomers that miniature replica "See Rock City" birdhouses are sold worldwide. Most of the original barns are but a memory. If you are lucky, you still may see one on America's backroads!

Mail Pouch Tobacco Barns--

Following the success of Rock City and Burma-Shave, other companies also rushed to paint their names on the rural landscape. This Mail Pouch Tobacco barn was spotted in Pennsylvania.

M. Barthel General Store, 1880--

The store's weathered cypress boards are bare of any paint, and the shelves still stocked with food supplies in this working general store which has appeared in many commercials and several movies.

Great River Road, S.R. 75, Sunshine, Louisiana

Prospect Mountain Diner--

Stainless steel diners were built in factories. Many had ID number plates over the entrance door, just like motor vehicles. Then shipped to location as one piece, or sometimes in two halves, with final assembly on location. Some of the largest diner factories were in New Jersey and Massachusetts, and so it's no wonder that the greatest number of steel diners ended up in the northeastern USA. Today only a fraction of them still exist, but when you find one, it can be a visual treat. Usually the food is a treat as well! -- *US 9, Lake George, New York.*

E.W. Hagwood General Store--

Back in 1900, a country doctor owned the store, and he had his doctor's office in the back. The post office was also inside the store. The town name of Causeyville was changed to Increase some years ago. The pine boards squeak as I walk through the old store, checking out the goods stored in wood barrels; and 1890s peanut roaster, the player piano and wood stove.

Increase (Causeyville), Mississippi

Chapter 11
Just Plain Silly!

On Texas highways, in construction zones, they post this sign: "State Law. Observe warning signs." Just who is this sign for? If you always observe road signs, then you don't need a sign telling you there is a state law that you must observe warning signs. And as for the fool who NEVER observes warning signs -- why do they think he will observe THIS sign?

What about the sign, "Deer crossing, next 1 mile." And then, "End deer crossing area." Who is this sign for? How do the deer know where the crossing area ends?

This chapter is just silly signs. Some were designed to be silly. Others may have been intended to be serious, but they all turned out silly. You decide which are which.
-L.E.

We reserve all comments on this!

Above: You're not lost, Loren. You are in downtown Hephzibah!

Hephzibah, Georgia

Right: This should help!

Top: Perhaps a better sign would be, "In downtown Intercourse."

S.R. 340 west of Intercourse, Pennsylvania

Center: "Moomaw Chevrolet customer parking." But look, not one of these vehicles is a Chevrolet!

Sugarcreek, Ohio

Bottom: My motto!

Nauvoo, Illinois

Left: Liquid fertilizer tank with a happy face.

Right: The international sign for "Watch for overturned trucks."

Below: *A bait shop in Northern Florida.*

Two Egg, Florida

There are several stories of how the tiny town of Two Egg got its name. The most popular is this: In this dusty town lived a large but poor black family. Each child owned one chicken, and he could barter the eggs at the general store. The eggs, in other words, were the kids' spending money.

Twice a week a "drummer," or traveling salesman, would come to sell supplies to the general store. Each time, he was amused by the line of barefoot children, each one bartering exactly two eggs.

When describing the town to a new associate, he said, "Oh, that's nothing but a Two-Egg town!" The associate, assuming it was the official town name, wrote "Two Egg" on the invoices, and the name stuck.

Two Egg, Florida

If you can read this, you're REALLY going the wrong way!

Rock Creek Lodge

Without getting too graphic here, let's just say that as bulls become steers, there is a surplus of testicles, or "Rocky Mountain Oysters." Deep fried, they are a western delicacy here at the Rock Creek Lodge. "Tastes like chicken."(I'll take their word for it, thank you.) Each September, Rock Creek Lodge hosts the Testicle Festival, featuring events such as wet T-shirt contests and hairy legs contests. (Let's hope the same person doesn't win both contests!)

Clinton, Montana

Yes, live bait "smelts." But it doesn't smelt as badly as dead bait, observes Loren. Sorry...

U.S. 1, Maine

Trout flies. Right. And canaries swim!

Maine

For people with 300 right feet!

There is at least one tavern in Dry Tavern, and it's not all dry! Caputo's Tavern serves great pizza, and ice-cold beer.

Dry Tavern, Pennsylvania

Basic human needs in Georgia!
U.S. 441, Tallulah Falls, Georgia

No thanks, I already had lunch!
U.S. 41, Tamiami Trail, Ochopee, Florida

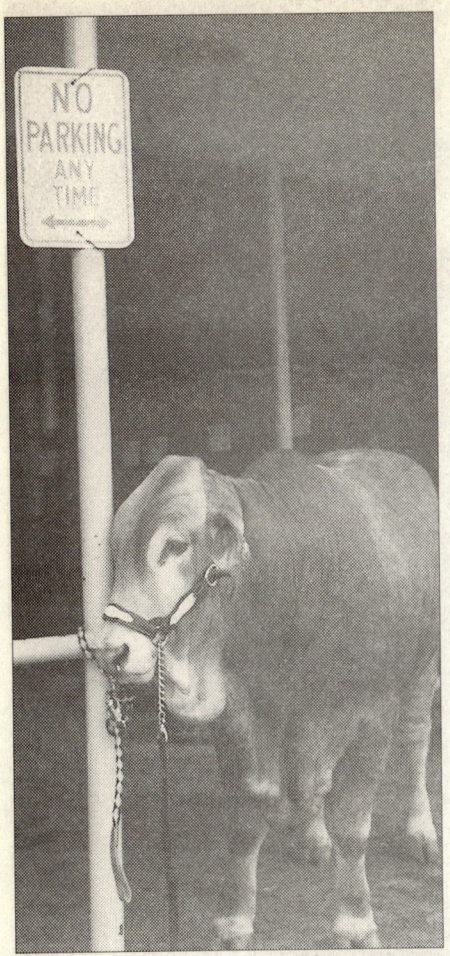

Wood carvings of silly bears.
 U.S. 93, Polson, Montana

U.S. 30, Nebraska

Above: Gatorland

U.S. 441, Kissimmee, Florida

A Corps of Engineers park and campground on the Arkansas River.

Conway, Arkansas

Kodak Cadillac--
A 1956 Cadillac covered with 35mm film canisters.
A camera shop on S.R. 60, Tampa Florida.

Big "er" small, they can help any animal!
Stuart, Florida

Happy Hooker charter fishing boat.

Key Largo, Florida

Leave your mittens at home; it's a Frost-Free Library.

Keene, New Hampshire

Frontier Days Parade.
Cheyenne, Wyoming

Pest control?
Pensacola, Florida

The Eleventh Commandment?

This cute sign has been duplicated at hundreds of churches, but it still gets a chuckle every time!

Watch out for Norman!

U.S. 95 Business, Coeur d-Alene, Idaho

An RV park near West Glacier, Montana.

Imagine that -- an OUTDOOR campground!

Hey, that's not a very nice comment about your cashier!

Tarpon Springs, Florida

The answer to the question, "My house is on fire, what should I do?"

Whynot, Mississippi

Above: Hurry, Unlimited time only!

Wow, look at the size of that "elk"!
Wall, South Dakota

Where do you go when you feel "Kaput"?
Deadwood, South Dakota

Carved bear
Bemidji, Minnesota

No snakes allowed, (except seeing-eye snakes!)
Lexington, South Carolina

Right: Well, if it's all the same to you, I'd prefer to bring them in dead!
Vidalia, Georgia

A sign of the times.
Campground in Central Florida.

"Don't confuse this with one of those cry-baby going out of business sales. We're going out of business FOREVER!"

Croom A Coochee, Florida
(near Lake Panasoffkee)

"All pottery must exit here!"
Myrtle Beach, South Carolina

Free funerals?

Unstable Fisherman's Organization.

S.R. 66 (old U.S. Route 66) Oklahoma

Bob sells only one book, and Bob is the author.

Frisco, Colorado

One honest businessman!

Welcome, sinners!
Florence, Alabama

Never again.
*U.S. 84,
Homerville, Georgia*

Burglar alarm!
Rod Cathcart's Dream Camper, Branson, Missouri.

Huh?

Left: Forrest Gump ahead!

Right: Maybe this is the slow traffic officer?
Upstate New York

Left: Call of the Wild Wildlife Museum.
C.R. 665, Ona, Florida

Chapter 12
Roadside Potpourri

One of the joys of a good roadtrip is watching for funny business slogans, bumper stickers, and personalized license plates. Here are just a few of my favorites:

SOME SLOGANS SPOTTED ON COMPANY TRUCKS:

In Miami: Ford draperies and verticals.
"Caution, a blind man is driving this truck."
In Fort Lauderdale: Three Star Auto Radiator.
"A good place to take a leak."
On every Waste Management truck in south Florida:
"Caution, this truck has bad breath." Also, *"Free snow removal."*
Batesville Casket Company.
"Please drive carefully, Heaven can wait."
Paschall Truck Lines.
"We drive a fine line."
In Moorhead City, NC: Gary Hill's Auto Radiator.
"Wanted--hot cars."
In south Florida, Johnson Septic Tank pumpout truck:
"It smells like money to me."
Name of a tool rental store in Deerfield Beach, Florida:
"Grand Rental Station."

BUMPER STICKERS:

On a luxury motorhome:
"We're spending the kid's inheritance."
On a wrecker:
"Tow-away zone."
"Humpty Dumpty was pushed."

Bumper sticker in south Florida:
"Thank you for not shooting."
On a Wisconsin farm truck:
"Support pork prices, run over a chicken."
On an Ohio pickup truck:
"Eat, sleep, go fishing."
On a Florida car:
"If Mama ain't happy, ain't nobody happy."
On an old Dodge Aspen in Mississippi:
"If I were an F-16, I'd be home by now."
On a Wisconsin car:
"Don't drink and drive -- you might hit a bump and spill it."
Another Wisconsin car:
"My ex-wife's car is a broom."
And finally, not a bumper sticker, but a woman's T-shirt:
"If they can send a man to the moon, why can't they send them all?"

VANITY TAGS:

FL. Someone very confident of his attraction to the opposite sex: *IMD14U*"
FL. On a convertible: -- *"JUS4SUN"*
FL. No doubt a retired police officer: -- *"WUZ FUZ"*
ME. On a red Mercedes roadster: -- *"HE PAID"*
FL. On a Rolls Royce: -- *"TOY 4 HIM"*
NY. -- *"Y WORRE"*
AL. On an RV: -- *"ROMAN"*
IL. -- *"YA GOOF"*
WI. On a minivan: -- *"MOM ETC"*
WI. On a Trans Am, bragging about an encounter with a Corvette: *"I 8 A VET"*
MD. -- *"I WANT $"*
NY. On a piano tuner's car: -- *"88 NOTES"*
IL. -- *"SLO N EZE"*
NC. Camaro: -- *"C MY RIDE"*
FL. -- *"NO SUSHI"*
IL. -- *"PAID IV"*
WI. -- *"B COOL"*
ON. Rolls Royce: -- *"MMMINE"*
VA. -- *"XQSE ME"*
VA. -- *"HUH Y E"*
VA. -- *"LOOK B4U"*
VA. On a Mustang: -- *"PET PONY"*
VA. -- *"HOME RN"*
VA. On a 300 ZX sports car: -- *"DAD'S MNY"*
VA. On a pickup truck: -- *"CATLFRMR"*
TN. Perhaps a heart surgeon: -- *"DFBUL8R"*
IL. -- *"ANGE RY 1"*
NY. On a Jeep: -- *"NO BRAKES"*
NC. On a Toyota: -- *"IN DEBT"*
NC. On a Volvo: -- *"XPNSV"*
VA. -- *"OY VEH"*
VA. -- *"I PLEZME"*

Chapter 13
Road Ends

Some of my favorite RV trips have been those where I follow one highway, end-to-end. Like US 41, with one end at Lake Superior in Michigan's Upper Peninsula and the other end at the Atlantic Ocean at Miami Beach. Or US 287, from the Gulf of Mexico at Port Arthur, Texas, to northern Montana. One thing you can count on -- all roads come to an end.

And so it is with books. I hope that you have enjoyed some of the back-road humor in this book. I hope that I haven't offended anyone. If even one or two of the photos brought a smile to your face, then I am happy. I'd enjoy hearing from you.

HOW CAN I FIND THESE PHOTO OPPORTUNITIES?

You may be wondering how one person can find so many silly signs; so many mailboxes; so many offbeat attractions?

Well, remember that I drove over 125,000 miles over a six-year period to find these. But you can train yourself to find roadside treasures.

1. Whenever possible, stay off the interstates, freeways, and tollways. Drive the secondary roads.

2. Take your time! I don't mean you should poke along at half the speed limit, but allow yourself enough time so that when you see something which might be a roadside nugget, you can stop and visit.

3. Don't drive after dark. Think of all you will miss if you can't see it!

4. Keep your eyes busy. Watch for cute mailboxes. Read the signs out loud; it will help to find signs with double meanings. If you are not sure it's funny, or misspelled, take a picture anyway. (I probably discard 1/3 of my photos after they are developed and only publish 5% of what I shoot.)

5. Have a notebook handy. If you can't stop and take a picture, make a note of what you saw. That funny vanity license plate, the funny signs. Make a scrapbook of your trip, complete with the park brochures, ticket stubs and snapshots. (If there are kids along, put them in charge of this.)

6. Avoid franchised food. Sample the local food! Some will be truly excellent. And I can guarantee, some will be truly bad! When that happens, make the best of it, and make a note in your scrapbook.

7. If you travel by car, try staying at some historic bed & breakfast inns. Try to find some of the little roadside cabins, and show the kids how we used to travel in the "old days!" If you are an RVer like me, maybe try some primitive national forest campgrounds, but balance it with some nights at private campgrounds.

ABOUT TWO-LANE ROADS QUARTERLY

All of the photographs in this book have appeared in one of the first 25 issues of *Two-Lane Roads,* my quarterly newspaper. Each issue contains about 100 photographs, plus human interest stories, and the RV lifestyle. Each of the journals is about 36 pages long, tabloid-size, black & white. Subscription rates in 1998 are $14 for one year (4 issues.) You may send that amount, and I will bill you for any price increases.

Please visit our website for subscription information, RV lifestyle info, Loren's appearance schedule, RV lifestyle books, plus much more.
http://www.two-lane.com

Or contact:
Two-Lane Roads • PO Box 23518 • Fort Lauderdale, FL 33307-3518
1-888-TWO-LANE

Autographed copies of this book can be obtained from the above sources, for US $10.95 plus shipping ($3 for one book, plus $1 for each additional) plus sales tax if your address is in Florida.